paperback heart
bill winchester

table of contents

paperback heart

i don't believe in much but i believe in you

when the bottles
are empty
and the cigarettes
lay in the ashtrays
like
tiny firecrackers
used up
in the morning

and
the bosses wait
and the sun
looks
down at us
with disappointment

we kiss,
do our best to brush
our teeth,
and then
jump in the river holding hands

love poems only
when you need them

i want to write something
for you about the
glory of
love,

something about
slow dances and
birth control,
about
the sweat that
never washes out of sheets

about the
mornings and
the late night
marathon drives
to cities
that look close on the
map
but are hours away
from the
two mattresses stacked in
the corner of the room

i want to get
it all into a single sentence
for you,
an arrow
lit
and fired
on an
irresponsible night

who wouldn't
love you?

you're out of reach
and on my mind,
you're self-conscious
but feel the need to speak
and you do
in your small voice,
saying nothing special
but still smiling
letting
beauty spill
out
onto your skin
from the wells
inside you
and
you have perfect posture
and you tug at your ponytail
making sure it touches your back just right,
and who wouldn't love you,
who gets to touch you
and
why aren't there fingerprints?

are you a joke

when i wake up
and think of your
small sneakers on
the sidewalk
and
when
the blinds do their best
to hold
the
morning back

and i brush my teeth and
think of
your thighs on
the passenger seat,
your teeth on my
neck,

your heart
on your sleeve

friday night poems

I taught myself
the piano because
I thought it would win
you back

I'm not
great
but neither
are you,

you flirt too
much
and don't
do the things
you say you'll
do,

your arms
are too long
and
you laugh too
easily

but I've got
this vision
of us sitting together
on the bench,
and I can fake
my way through
a few things,

come on
over

i like
you

you can build love like
music and fire,

explain the shape
of falling water,

you can
watch the
dust strain through sunlight

what i
need

i bet i could put you
on my shoulders
and you'd like it
i bet we could close a city of bars
and
waste a lifetime of mornings

i bet it'd feel good to look into
uncertain,
intelligent eyes;
you seem like
the kind of trouble
i need

mercy

meet me on the mississippi
with a bottle
meet me with your wet hair
and a movie star smile
meet me with
marching bands
and eyes filled
to the tip
with strange sadness

leave your brain far behind
and
meet me in the wet
streets of new orleans

too many love poems

i'll fall in love too
easily
and for almost no reason
at all
it's hilarious
to feel
a heart
stop on a dime
a
slow dance off
a cliff
and
lips
too good
at things
lips weren't made to
do

too many love poems
for two skinny arms

and
the newspaper
on the
mat in
the morning

close to
the edge

we push ourselves
farther
towards the edge

watching the humorless
and the tragic
sail right past us
and over
and down

we share a couch,
a box of cereal,
a lifestyle

we share
what we've managed
to steal
and hide

8 AM, Wednesday

our love
is
a bar
that doubles as a
planetarium

it is
the zoo
after hours

it is the empty
theater
where they let
the movie run

it is
hands that touch
reaching for
the same
book;

our love runs naked
down the street
with sparklers,
8 AM, Wednesday

it's
good

it's odd to find someone
without having to look

someone
where words
aren't necessary,
where
being there is all you really need
and when they're not there,
they are there
somehow

and it's
good

whole

we are magnets
finally
snapped
back together,
unbalanced
atoms
sorting themselves
out
at 4AM

currents
recharging
worn-out souls
as we sleep—

two halves
and one

whole

with each
breath

with each breath
you heal the
earth,
you heal the
air that
hangs heavy
and
thick above
lonely heads,
you take it in
and it comes back out
a little better,
electric,
a
part of you

impulsive

we got up
out of the booth
thinking
one would call
the other's bluff

but i got in the car
and then you did
and i pointed the car
in the direction
of the coast
and you didn't stop me

a few hours later
we were
there

so we walked the beach
until we decided to go back

and the
waves grabbed
the footprints
the laughter
and the
night

spark

when you bring me your love
don't use teaspoons,
use a pitchfork

and don't
use your words,
use your hands

and when your
feet swing off my bed
and touch
the ground,
be sure they
spark

i write
for you

i write for you
in a blizzard,
small words,
anxieties and
disappointments,
glasshouse love
and flat-footed reason

i write for you
all the time,
until my fingers
miss the keys,
until the rain hails
and the cab comes

this is
your poem

I've spent months
trying to figure out
how to get
you down
on paper

I've tilted bottles
and paid tabs
I've stared
strained
slept
and
gambled

I've met the sun
with
empty glassy
eyes
on the edge of a bed
of someone
I barely
know

but you've always been
on my mind

a puzzle

something washed up
on the shore

and on
the tip
of my
tongue

your glow

I want you,

your smile,
your body,
your love,
I want it
all

and
every night,

I want to watch
your
perfection
glow
in the dark

sweeping up
the stars

under our blankets,
with your body warm
and the midnight
hanging
tough
and
tired
between us
our young souls

resting on their laurels
while
creation hums around us—

explosions that
silently rock the
empty space
and the brilliant
show it
leaves behind

paperback
heart

I have a paperback
heart
dog-eared and creased
by the world,

the colors
are faded
and the spine is worn
but I'm glad
to see
it's finally in
good
hands

worn

lay with me
in the late morning,
decommissioned,
exhausted,
bearing the weight
of a neurotic
world,

lay your heavy head
next to mine,
your tender body
one slice of
an ancient
soul

and in the morning
when the night melts off

and in the morning
when the
night melts off
and you
run
the shower
and I leave
to do
the things I need
to do

I start the car
and the song that
was cut short
with the engine
the night before
comes to life
again
but it
has no more power,
it is
a cartoon,
it is thin,
it is worthless

and I head
out into the pink
light,

I switch the turn
signal on
and
do my best to
wait

daydreams

when the nights
are long
and the days
are
empty

i think of your
bed and
body,

your
small sounds
through
parted
lips--

it's the
daydreams
that wake me
from
the nightmares

she's trained
the birds

she's trained the birds
to rise with
the sun,

given them reason
to sing
and
meter to their song,

she's in the
scent of
coffee,

at least in
my coffee,
that I brew in
no special
way

the wasted june

we laid
tattooed,
unfocused
and
discrete
in
a month without
slammed doors,
woke up
with the
mail truck
and felt
nervous about
checking
the box
it was
cattle
shot
and branded,
cotton candy
in the
sunset,
satellites
and
dollar bills
on fire
sirens,
paper bags,
soft-serve,
and

limelight
until we
were full,
finally
thrilled with
ourselves

you make stupid
decisions

you
make stupid
decisions

you wait for
near strangers
in parking lots

give the
finger
to cabs

you're crazy

certifiably

but if you called me
I'd drive across
5 states

without
thought

I'd stop at gas stations
at 4 AM

I'd fight through
bad sports talk
and the
rockies

i'd make it.

easy.

and
you'd jump in
the car
1AM monday
and

say,

"baby,

where are
we
going?"

what
i know

sometimes i feel
like i know everything i
need to know
drawing the curtains on the
morning
and watching the steam rise off
the cold city

i can feel things
that are beyond my
reason

watching the first
car crawl
across the waiting
pavement

i feel
something electric

as you walk
back into the bedroom,
your voice repairing
a broken
melody

knots

there are accidental
knots
made between people

knots that boats
and
shoelaces can't use

knots that make
near strangers
spoon-feed you soft-serve ice cream
and
get them glasses of water
in the middle of the night

knots that are so
complicated
that you can never
really get them all the way
out

ashes

it's entertaining
to watch fireworks,
rockets;
controlled explosions

but as soon
as they become
unpredictable
they become
unsettling
and
the awe
turns into
panic;

that's the problem with us,
we are fireworks
one minute
and the next we are
forrest fires,
solar flares,
cigarettes
and we burn
wild and
reckless
until late at night,

when i fall
heavy
next
to you
in bed

we don't need love

we don't need love to keep us together,
there's lust
and insecurity
and sympathy
and jealousy
and pity
and shame
and denial
and laziness
and guilt
and uncertainty
and fear

and
even with only one of those,
I think we can make it
just fine

the hours, minutes, and seconds

love me now
before
the drinks take our bodies
before
the jobs take our heart
before
the sadness takes our mind

before
god takes back the sky

while you
were out

I've written you
rock n roll love songs
on liquor store
receipts

and I've
filled my bedside
table with
endless cups of
coffee

I've lived near the edge
with unfiltered cigarettes,
used cars,
and thin walls

I've stood on
balconies
with
skinny
crazy
girls
wired on
failure
and
booze

and I've
drank to you
on silent weekend nights
staring
at the ceiling

I've driven for miles
without
destination
listening to
worn out songs

and arrived one more time
at your
door

two of
a kind

what choice do
we have
when
the world has
shuffled us up like
this,

when we end up
two
hearts
on top of
another,
dealt to the
same shaking
hand—

two of a kind
among
what
appears to
do us
no
good.

a broken heart
is nothing new

a broken heart is nothing new,
nothing interesting
or even exciting,
it's just a thing,
an expected thing
like the weather,
good or bad,
something shiny
to take her hand
and walk her
away

and
god bless you
and your
funny ways,
god bless the
hopeless moments
when you show up at my
door
like a lost cat
or angel—

bad news
wrapped in
some other
guy's
coat

the average
love affair

it's been tough between us,
probably more
unfair
than the average
love affair

and that's unfortunate
but not unbearable

and to be honest
it's mostly your
fault

you can't make
your mind up
over
anything
and it's
hard to
deal with someone
like that.

the joy you bring me
is inconvenient
and

i'll light
a cigar
and lean back
in my chair,
feet on
my wide
and empty desk

when your
heart
finally
tugs
at my sleeve.

the
hard nights

it seemed like
ending it
was the smart thing;

that
we would become
better,
maybe even
functional
people

that we would be able
to do normal
things
like buy new tires
or
change the
air filter

and that may
be
true

but when
i get home
from the bar
and
see

no messages,
one toothbrush,
and
an empty bed

i don't want to be normal

the girl on
the couch

why aren't you across from me
why aren't you on the couch
while i'm on this chair typing
why don't you have a bottle of wine on the floor
and why isn't
the light low
and
where is the
slow country music
where are the endless parties
and
the late mornings
and
why did i wake up without you

minutes

two miles above sea
level
I can still hear you

I can't clear my
head
and I feel like
I'm losing more of
myself
every day

I'm surrounded by
strange christmas trees
and dying wildflowers
and
there are sorority girls
screaming
about
the weather
and
where they're going to
eat for lunch
and you're
across this state and
a few others

and
I'm here
in a parking lot
with a cup of
bad coffee

weighed down by
thousands of
minutes of
heartache,

no match for
the mountains

and I might not see you stretched out on the bed again

you're on my mind
for the first time
in months
and I know
that if I sat down
and wrote about
you
the
re-examining of images
and moments
and the frustration of
trying to come up with
the right words
would
get rid of those inconvenient
thoughts

but
I think I'll
save it
for another
day

nothing, really

i was never
impressed with
new york or
la
like i was
impressed with
you,
and

nothing's really
put out
the wildfires
you lit
years ago
with
your
dark eyes
and

your skinny wrists
on my
shoulders,

nothing's
filled in
that
series of
small,
dangerous
footprints

you tracked across
my
bed,

nothing
at
all

searching

i've tried bars
and bus stations

the most famous parks
in the biggest
cities
on the brightest days

and i've wandered
the most
hidden streets
on rainy nights

i know it's there

because i saw it
once

in your eyes

wherever
you are

you
laid on the
floor,
your toes pointing due east
while I sat on the couch

you looked
destroyed,
abandoned,
and beautiful
and
all I
could think of to do was
to get more ice from the freezer

so I dropped a fresh cube in
each of our
red plastic cups...

and baby,
wherever you are,
if you're having a hard time
I promise that
if you can make it through
the night

the morning will be better

the balcony

there was a balcony
next to a neon sign
there were
endless cigarettes
endless bottles of wine
endless laughter
it was just a balcony
but with you
it was the
top of the
eiffel tower
in a hurricane

I saw you yesterday
for the first time in years
you were
coming back from a new job
coming home to a new bed
coming home to someone else
your eyes were still
brilliant and heartbreaking
but that person
who laughed on the balcony
who brought the minutes in with
tiny explosions
was
gone

I pray
I'll be lucky enough
to find you again
in someone else

living on nothing at all

every now and then
I'll look back
on the empty days I spent
with you
and feel a tug in the
back of my mind,
the back of my heart,
the back of my throat

and every once in a while
I get the urge to live
like that again
but
I'm too old for that kind of thing,
I'd start to feel bad about myself
and besides I don't think
I could find anyone that would come close
to matching your infamous company—
your raging beauty
drunk on simplicity,
floating
a hair's width
above your
lucky
sheets

a
moment

i can imagine our conversation
months from now:
"i still think about you/yeah, me too/i didn't throw your
toothbrush away/me neither/i met someone/me too/i hope
you're happy/me too/i'll never forget the good stuff/me
neither/i'll see you sometime/definitely"

but we never will,
we will gradually forget
and meet people a little bit closer
to ourselves
and become people we had no intention of becoming
and on rare drunk nights
we will remember
with just the right
amount of sadness
the rare spark
that we lit
for a moment

my dreams
of you

my dreams of you
drop like ink into
water,
blossoming
and
twisting
into shapes beyond
reason,
failing and creating
on the edge of
brilliance
until finally
the water
grays

you do your best

it's happened to everyone
and it will happen again

it's why people
play the accordion
or
stare at the red numbers
of the bedside clock

and
you can't really fix it,
it stays with you

but it makes you better

because
when you step up to
the plate the next time
you'll be smarter
and
quicker

you'll know
the right angles
and instincts,

you'll know
when to give
and what to give
and how to take

you'll be
a genius,

the master
of
your heart

under
the rising sun

i could waste time
writing about
love lost but
i'd rather
spend my mornings
with coffee
remembering there's
love waiting--

voices that need
new names to speak
and new
promises to keep,

skin that
needs
new
hands,

and
souls that need
new
light

i saw
you

you looked good

like you're finally becoming the
person you were meant to be

like
you have found a
balance between
how to give the
world what it needs

and how to
hold on
to what you
need.

i saw you

farther from the
edge
and

you looked good.

30841284R00046